**HE**

CW00733675

My name is Professor Callidus, but my friends call me 'the Professor'. I've spent years digging in the desert for ancient and valuable treasures.

But the funny thing is, one of my most valuable treasures wasn't buried in the desert at all. It's my Bible, and I found it in a bookshop! I've got a modern copy, but it's actually a very ancient book. And it's fascinating! Not just because of all the interesting history and exciting stories in it, but because it tells us all about God too. So I've written this notebook to help you explore the Bible for yourself.

Happy exploring!

The Professor.

Psst! It's best to start at the beginning and do the pages in order.

The Bible library, Part 1

Did you know that the word 'Bible' means 'library'? The Bible isn't just one book; it's a collection of 66 different books.

The first 39 books are in a section called the Old Testament, and the other 27 are the New Testament. But all these books are part of one big story – God's story!

Psst! Use the contents page at the front of your Bible to fill in the missing Old Testament books.

GENESIS · EXODUS · LEVITICUS · DEUTERONOMY · JOSHUA · JUDGES · RUTH · 1 SAMUEL · 2 SAMUEL · 1 KINGS · 1 CHRONICLES

2 CHRONICLES · EZRA · NEHEMIAH · ESTHER · JOB · PSALMS · ECCLESIASTES · S OF SONGS · ISAIAH · JEREMIAH · LAMENTATIONS

EZEKIEL · DANIEL · HOSEA · JOEL · AMOS · OBADIAH · MICAH · NAHUM · HABAKKUK · ZEPHANIAH · HAGGAI · ZECHARIAH · MALACHI

A really good shorthand!

The books in the Bible are set out really cleverly. Each book is divided into small sections, called 'chapters'. And each chapter is split up into 'verses' of a few words or sentences.

So instead of writing out whole Bible stories in my notebook, I can just write the book, chapter and verse. For example, **Genesis 2:1** means 'Genesis, chapter 2, verse 1'. Brilliant!

You might want to practise this shorthand. Look up these verses and write down what they say.

Genesis 2:1

_____

Exodus 20:3

_____

Answers:

Do not worship any god except me.

So the heavens and the earth and everything else were created.

In the beginning

The first five books in the Bible tell us about God's promises to his people and about the agreement he made with them. As part of the agreement God gave them some laws to keep. So this part of the Bible library is called the Law section.

The first book is called **Genesis**, which is quite appropriate really because 'genesis' means 'beginning'!

Read **Genesis 1:1–2:4**. God made the world in just six days! Can you write or draw the things God made each day?

Day 1 verses 3–5
_____

Day 2 verses 6–8
_____

Day 3 verses 9–13
_____

Day 4 verses 14–19
_____

Day 5 verses 20–23
_____

Day 6 verses 24–31
_____

Day 7 chapter 2 verses 2–4
_____

Law

A sneaky snake!

I got a terrible fright once when a snake went up my trouser leg! Snakes can be very troublesome, even for people not wearing trousers!

Have a look at **Genesis 3:1–8**.

Find the key words to discover what spoils God's world. It's in the shaded boxes.

The sneakiest and most cunning animal.

The woman disobeyed God and ate the…

Then she gave some to her…

Law

When you've worked out the answer, you might need to interview an adult to find out what it means. Then look at

Genesis 3:22–24 to see what happened next.

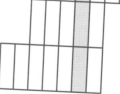

The ship of the desert

The camel is often called the 'ship of the desert'. A camel can go for days without water, but a real ship can't of course! So why would anybody want to build a ship on dry land?

Read **Genesis 6:11–7:10** to find out.

Hear from God

Who built a boat far away from the sea?

_____

How big was the boat?

_____

And what did it carry?

_____

You can see that God really hates sin. But look at **Genesis 9:8–13** for some good news.

Draw God's special sign here, using the right colours if you have them.

What's in a name?

As I explore, the names **Abram** and **Abraham** keep cropping up. There's another name too: **Canaan**.

Read each passage, then tick the names it mentions.

	Abram	Abraham	Canaan
Genesis 12:1–2	☐	☐	☐
Genesis 15:1–6	☐	☐	☐
Genesis 17:1–8	☐	☐	☐

What have you found out about Abram and Abraham?

_____

And what does the name Canaan refer to?

_____

Can you add the missing names? **Genesis 25:19–26** will help you.

Abraham's son was called _____.
He married _____.
  Their twin sons were called _____
    and _____.

Law

7

Joseph

Some of the inscriptions I find have difficult words to translate. I have to choose the most likely word to fit in with the rest.

Here is the story of Joseph. Can you choose the right words?

Jacob had 12 sons, but he **loved/hated** Joseph the most. So Joseph's brothers **loved/hated** Joseph. **(Genesis 37:3–4)**

They threw Joseph into a **dry well/dungeon/river**. Then they **sent/sold/gave** Joseph to some traders, who took him to **Egypt/Babylon**. **(Genesis 37:23–28)**

Joseph helped the king to understand some **recipes/maths/dreams**, so the king made Joseph a **cake/governor**. **(Genesis 41:32–41)**

Joseph had two **sons/daughters/goldfish** called Manasseh and Ephraim. **(Genesis 41:50–52)**

Later, Jacob and his whole family went to **Egypt/Babylon** to live with Joseph. **(Genesis 46:1–7)**

Law

Tribes of slaves

Can you find the list of names hidden inside this puzzle? **Exodus 1:1–5** might give you a clue. When you find the hidden names, cross them out and write them here.

N	T	R	B	H	D	E	R
A	N	R	E	H	S	A	A
P	M	E	N	U	H	S	G
H	S	H	J	C	B	O	F
T	A	I	A	I	V	E	L
A	D	S	M	D	L	L	N
L	S	A	I	E	U	T	H
I	E	S	N	J	O	J	N
S	O	F	J	A	C	N	O
N	U	L	U	B	E	Z	B

The unused letters will tell you whose names they are.

Exodus starts about 400 years after Jacob and his family went to live in Egypt. In that time, Joseph's brothers' families had grown really big. They were so big that each brother had a whole tribe of descendants.

Now read **Exodus 1:6–11** to see what happened next.

Treasure in the Nile

A lot of the treasures I find were once hidden away to keep them safe. What would you hide if there was danger about? Many years ago in Egypt, something very precious was hidden...

Read **Exodus 1:22 – 2:10** to see what was hidden, and where.

Colour in the shapes with dots to see what's hidden in the long grass.

Law

What was the baby's name? _____

Who adopted him? _____

_____

Plagues

When Moses grew up, God sent him to tell the king to let God's people leave Egypt. Moses took his brother Aaron and told the king what God said. But the king refused to let the slaves go.

Draw the things God did to make the king change his mind.

Exodus 7:19–20	Exodus 8:5–6	Exodus 8:16–17
Exodus 8:24	Exodus 9:6–7	Exodus 9:8–9
Exodus 9:17–19	Exodus 10:13–14	Exodus 10:21–22

Read **Exodus 11:10.** Did the king let the people go? **Yes/No**

Escape from Egypt

I've been to Egypt many times. I'm quite well known there and I can come and go as I please. But the Israelites couldn't, because they were the Egyptians' slaves. They needed someone to save them.

Read **Exodus 12:29–36**
Use the same three letters to complete each sentence. (H _ _ _ fun!)

The Israelites were sl _ _ _ s in Egypt. Br _ _ _ Moses told the king to let them le _ _ _. After some gr _ _ _ disasters the king finally allowed them to tr _ _ _ l away from Egypt. The Egyptians even g _ _ _ them gold and silver. God had s _ _ _ d his people!

Read **Exodus 13:21–22**.
Draw a picture of God guiding the Israelites.

Law

A dry sea

Have you ever decided something, but then changed your mind about it? After the Israelites had left Egypt, the king changed his mind about letting them go. So he chased them with his army. The Israelites found themselves trapped between the Egyptians and the sea!

Hear from God

Read **Exodus 14:21–29**.
Can you spot the differences between these pictures?

God is so powerful he can do anything! **WOW!**

13

God's rules

Can you think of any rules you have to keep? Are the rules helpful? God gave his people some very good rules.

Hear from God

Read **Exodus 20:1–17**. Circle the rules about God. Underline the rules about how to treat other people.

1 Do not worship any god except me.
2 Don't bow down and worship idols.
3 Do not misuse my name.
4 Keep the seventh day holy.
5 Respect your father and your mother.
6 Do not murder.
7 Be faithful in marriage.
8 Do not steal.
9 Do not tell lies about others.
10 Do not want anything that belongs to someone else.

These rules are just as important today. Ask God to help you to keep them.

Talk with God

Law

The sacred chest

Where do you keep your important things? In a cupboard? Under your bed? When I'm travelling, I have a special case to keep all my treasures safe. It's not as special as the Israelites' sacred chest though!

Hear from God

Why was it so special? Read **Exodus 25:10–22** to find out!

This drawing of the sacred chest hasn't been finished.

☀ Add the measurements of the sides.

☀ Draw in the other parts of the box.

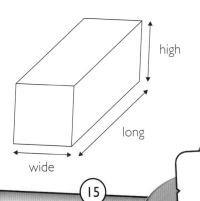

high

long

wide

Law

A secret report

When I go to explore a new country, I check it out first so I know what to expect. That's what the Israelites did when they reached the country that God had promised to give them. They sent 12 spies to check it out.

Hear from God

Read **Numbers 13:23–14:9**.

Use the Israelites' code to read what the spies said.

I	S	R	A	E	L	B	C	D	F	G	H	J	K	M	N	O	P	Q	T	U	V	W	X	Y	Z
A	B	C	D	E	F	G	H	I	J	K	L	M	N	O	P	Q	R	S	T	U	V	W	X	Y	Z

TCMQE NEMNHE IPE JURCTMM QTPMKB LMP UQ

_____

But what did Joshua and Caleb say?

TCE HMPA DQ MK MUP QDAE, IKA TCEY WMK'T
QTIKA I RCIKRE IBIDKQT UQ!

_____

Talk with God

Ask God to help you to trust him, especially when things seem really tough.

Law

16

The History books

The next set of books is the History section. It tells us what happened after the people arrived in Canaan, the land that God had promised them. Do you like history at school? The History books in the Bible are really exciting. There are stories of heroes and villains, love and romance, and kings and battles. And they're all true! In fact, that's why I became an archaeologist – so that I could find out all about them.

JOSHUA | JUDGES | RUTH | 1 SAMUEL | 2 SAMUEL | 1 KINGS

2 KINGS | 1 CHRONICLES | 2 CHRONICLES | EZRA | NEHEMIAH | ESTHER

It doesn't add up

If something doesn't make sense, we often say "that doesn't add up". So, you might say this if someone said they could walk on the ceiling, run faster than a train or knock a wall down by shouting at it!

When Moses died, Joshua took over as leader. Remember Joshua's report? He wanted to enter the land God had promised. But there was a walled city called Jericho in the way!

Hear from God

Read **Joshua 6:2–20**. If God says something, it always adds up!

Can you make this sum add up?

The number of priests
carrying the trumpets: _____

The number of days when +
they walked round once a day: _____

The number of times they +
walked around on day seven: _____

                                    20

History

God's maths again!

The Israelites settled in Canaan, but other countries still attacked them sometimes. When that happened, God chose people to lead the Israelites. They were called judges and there's a Bible book all about them.

One judge was called Gideon and his enemies were called the Midianites.

 Read **Judges 7:1–8.** How many soldiers did Gideon think he needed? (Add the two numbers in verse 3) _____

But how many did God say he needed? (verses 6–7)

_____

Read verse 12. Draw an X on the sword to show how many soldiers the Midianites had.

Just a few   Loads!

 Read **Judges 7:19–22** to see what happened.

The Midianites were defeated. God had saved his people again! **WOW!**

History

Other judges

There were lots of judges. Look up their names and then find them in the wordsearch. Gideon is there too.

Judges 3:9   O _ _ _ _ _ _
Judges 3:15   E _ _ _
Judges 3:31   S _ _ _ _ _
Judges 4:4   D _ _ _ _ _
Judges 10:1–2   T _ _ _
Judges 10:3   J _ _ _
Judges 12:7   J _ _ _ _ _ _
Judges 12:8–10   I _ _ _ _
Judges 12:11–12   E _ _ _
Judges 12:13–15   A _ _ _ _
Judges 16:31   S _ _ _ _ _
1 Samuel 7:15–16 S _ _ _ _ _

A	P	K	A	L	O	T	R
N	O	E	D	I	G	L	J
P	O	T	H	N	I	E	L
N	P	S	A	U	P	U	N
J	O	Z	M	H	D	M	O
A	B	D	T	A	J	A	L
I	I	H	B	I	S	S	E
R	A	G	M	A	H	S	Q
H	A	R	O	B	E	D	W

The people ask for a king

I've explored lots of kings' palaces, statues and tombs. They are usually very grand, because kings liked to show their power. But when the Israelites asked God for a king, the man God chose was much more shy.

Hear from God

Read **1 Samuel 10:17–25** to see what happened.

Find the message hidden amongst the bags. Then compare your answer with **1 Samuel 9:17** (The words have been taken from the CEV Bible. They may not be exactly the same as the words in your Bible).

The Lord told satchel Samuel, this kitbag is the rucksack man handbag I told you briefcase about. He's the one suitcase who will holdall rule Israel carrier-bag.

King David

I don't always have to go to dusty deserts and ancient ruins to see treasures. I saw a statue of King David in Florence in Italy. (It was nice to eat pizza for a change instead of sandwiches!) David became King of Israel after King Saul died.

Hear from God Read **2 Samuel 7:8–16** to find out what God promised David.

Join up the words in the right order. What shape appears?

make   that •

• be   I   one •

• always   king   will   • sure

• will   descendents   your   of •

King David made Jerusalem his capital city and he built his palace there. When David died, his son Solomon became king, as God had promised.

King Solomon

If you could have anything you wanted, what would you ask for? Money? Fame? Happiness? The latest games console? When God asked King Solomon what he wanted, he didn't ask for any of these things.

Hear from God

Read **1 Kings 3:1–15** to see what he did ask for.

Here's King Solomon's 'shopping' list.

☀ Draw a circle around the things Solomon asked God for.

☀ Underline the things Solomon didn't ask for but God gave him anyway.

☀ Cross out the rest.

riches
long life milk
enemies destroyed
greatness

wisdom
long life
teabags
God's blessing

Talk with God

Ask God to give you wisdom too, so that you can make right decisions.

Wisdom and poetry

As well as Law and History, the Bible has five books of poems, songs and wise sayings.

Job is a long poem about a man called Job who stayed faithful to God even when things got tough.

JOB

Psalms are poems and songs about God. King David wrote a lot of them. Psalms is the longest book in the Bible.

PSALMS

Proverbs are wise sayings. King Solomon wrote many of these proverbs.

PROVERBS

Ecclesiastes is a preacher's thoughts about life.

ECCLESIASTES

Song of Songs is sometimes called Song of Solomon. It's a collection of songs and poems about love.

S OF SONGS

Rebellion!

When King Solomon died, his son Rehoboam became king. But Rehoboam did not listen to his people and he treated them cruelly.

Hear from God

Read **1 Kings 12:15–21** to see how the people reacted.

Colour in the tribes that revolted. They became a new country and they called themselves Israel. Only two tribes stayed loyal to King Rehoboam, Judah and Benjamin. (The tribe of Benjamin was soon absorbed by Judah.) Colour them in a different colour.

ASHER

NAPHTALI

DAN

MANASSEH

ZEBULUN

ISSACHAR

MANASSEH

GAD

EPHRAIM

DAN

BENJAMIN

REUBEN

JUDAH

The Prophets

Both countries, Israel and Judah, disobeyed God. So God sent messengers, called prophets, to tell them to obey him. All of these books (apart from Lamentations) are the names of prophets.

Some of the prophets had messages for Israel and some had messages for Judah. Some even had messages for other countries too. But the books aren't arranged in place order or date order. They're in order of size.

ISAIAH JEREMIAH LAMENTATIONS EZEKIEL DANIEL

HOSEA JOEL AMOS OBADIAH JONAH MICAH NAHUM HABAKKUK ZEPHANIAH HAGGAI ZECHARIAH MALACHI

The first five Prophecy books are the biggest, so they're called the major prophets. The other smaller books are called the minor prophets.

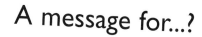

A message for...?

I'd like to find out more about these prophets, but I'll need to know where to dig. Can you draw lines to link the prophets with the places they lived or had messages for? Look at the first few verses of their books for clues.

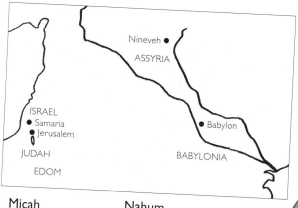

Micah

Nahum

Jonah

Haggai

Obadiah

Ezekiel

Isaiah

Jeremiah

Prophets

The northern kingdom

The people of the northern kingdom, Israel, kept disobeying God.

Read **Amos 5:14** to see what the prophet told them.

Stop _____

and start _____.

Here are some of the things they did. Can you unjumble them? **Hosea 4:1–3** might help you.

SILE _____

RUM RED _____

BERRY BO _____

RUN CIGS _____

VILE ONCE _____

YES NOT DISH _____

God said he would punish the northern kingdom. Read **2 Kings 17:5–6** to see where they vanished to.

Add Amos and Hosea to the map on page 27 and draw lines to link them to Israel. Then draw an arrow from Israel to Assyria to show where the people were taken.

Prophets

The southern kingdom

Hear from God
Read **Jeremiah 13:1–11** and you'll see why I hardly ever find treasures made of cloth.

The southern kingdom of Judah wasn't destroyed when Israel was. But God said it would be destroyed if the people kept disobeying him. They would become like Jeremiah's shorts.

Change the picture to show what happened to the shorts.

Hear from God
Read **2 Kings 25:1–12** to see what happened to Judah and its capital, Jerusalem.

King N_____ of B_____
captured J_____.

The people of Judah were taken to Babylonia. On the map on page 27, draw an arrow from Judah to Babylonia.

Prophets

Two sticks

I got lost in the desert once. I ended up miles away from where I wanted to be, but I knew I'd get back to the right place in the end.

God's people were miles away from their own country, but prophets like Jeremiah, Ezekiel and Daniel prayed for them and promised that one day they would be able to go back.

Hear from God

Read **Ezekiel 37:15–28**.
Write the countries' names on the two sticks. Draw a hand holding them in the middle so that they look like one stick.

Not long after King Nebuchadnezzar died, Babylonia was defeated by King Cyrus of Persia. Read **Ezra 1:1–7** to see what happened then.

Psst! 'Israel' now means both Israel and Judah.)

Prophets

The temple rebuilt

Did you notice that the Prophecy and History books overlap? The prophets weren't separate from the history of God's people, they were part of it! So we need to go back to the History section to carry on the story...

Read **Ezra 3:7–13**
Can you read this word to see what they built?

FOUNDATIONS

The other people in the area caused trouble and stopped the building. But then some prophets encouraged them to start again.

Read **Ezra 5:1–2** and **6:14**.

Who encouraged them? H_____
and Z_____.

Do you recognise these two names? They both have books in the Prophecy section of the Bible. Add Zechariah to your map on page 27 and link him to Jerusalem.

The walls rebuilt

Not all of the Israelites had returned to Judah with Zerubbabel and the others. Some, like Nehemiah, stayed behind in Persia. In fact, Nehemiah was the Persian king's personal servant. But he still thought about Jerusalem…

Hear from God

Read **Nehemiah 2:1–20**

Unjumble the words:

Before he asked people to help him, Nehemiah PER DAY _____ and

PEN LAND _____.

Can you work out how many bricks are in this pile? It's the same as the number of days it took to rebuild the walls. You can check your answer in **Nehemiah 6:15**.

The Bible library, Part 2

The second part of the Bible is called the New Testament. It tells us how God made a new agreement with his people, in a very special way! The first four books of the New Testament are called 'Gospels', which means 'good news'!

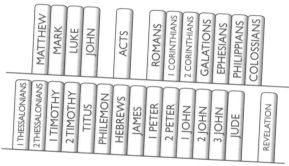

The New Testament story starts over 400 years after the Old Testament story ends. During that time the Persian empire was taken over by the Greek king, Alexander the Great. Later still, Jerusalem and Israel became part of the Roman empire. But the people hoped that one day God would send someone to save them…

Hark! The herald angel!

Do you like Christmas? I do. Mrs Professor usually gives me a new spade. One year I spent Christmas in the jungle and we had roast snake instead of turkey for dinner. That was quite unusual!

But the first ever Christmas was very, very unusual…

Hear from God

Read **Luke 1:26–38**
Give each person the right label.

Gospels

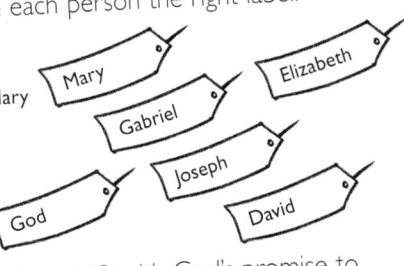

engaged to marry Mary
Mary's relative
Jesus' father
Jesus' ancestor
Jesus' mother
an angel

Mary   Elizabeth   Gabriel   Joseph   God   David

Compare verses 32 and 33 with God's promise to King David (on page 22).

WOW!

God was going to keep his promise in a way that King David could never have expected!

Tests in the desert

The things I dig up in the desert are often damaged or broken. But every now and then, I find a real treasure that's perfect in every way.

Jesus went into a desert when he was about thirty years old.

Read **Matthew 4:1–11** to see what happened.

Who tested Jesus? _____

But Jesus didn't do wrong, because he obeyed God's rules from the Law section of the Bible.

Can you match up these verses?

1 Matthew 4:4   a **Deuteronomy 6:13**
2 Matthew 4:7   b **Deuteronomy 8:3**
3 Matthew 4:10   c **Deuteronomy 6:16**

Gospels

Jesus was perfect. He never ever did anything sinful! **WOW!**

Ask God to help you to be strong when you are tempted to do wrong.

Talk with God

35

Jesus the storyteller

Jesus told lots of interesting stories to teach people about God. These are some of my favourites, because they involve people who might use a spade… like me!

Hear from God

What might the people in these stories use a spade for?

Matthew 7:24–29 _____

Matthew 13:44 _____

Luke 13:6–9 _____

Luke 13:18–19 _____

Choose one of these stories and draw a picture of it.

The lost sheep: **Luke 15:4–7**. The good Samaritan: **Luke 10:30–37**. The sower: **Mark 4:3–8 (and 13–20)**.

Gospels

Jesus does amazing things

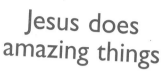

I'm amazed that the ancient Egyptians could build pyramids. But the things Jesus did are much, much more amazing – they're miracles!

Healing miracles

What parts of the body did Jesus heal in these four stories.

1 Matthew 9:2–7 _____   2 Mark 7:31–37 _____
3 Luke 6:6–10 _____   4 John 9:1–7 _____

Other miracles

How many fish?

Matthew 17:24–27	Luke 9:12–17	John 21:1–11

___ + ___ + ___ = ___ **?**

Jesus did lots of other miracles too and there was nothing 'fishy' about any of them. He could really do these things because he is God's Son!

WOW!

Jesus enters Jerusalem

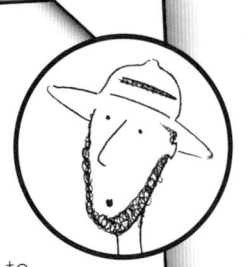

I've seen lots of carvings from different ancient countries. These show that when generals won important battles, they used to parade through the streets while the people cheered them.

Read **Matthew 21:1–11**

Who hasn't put their cloak on the road?

It seems the people thought Jesus was going to win an important military battle too. Perhaps they hoped he'd beat the Romans.

Jesus eats with friends

How do you remember things? I usually tie my neck scarf on to my shovel. Then when I see it I know that there's something I need to remember. And if that doesn't work I remember when I get sand down my neck!

Luke 22:14–23 tells us about something to remind us of Jesus.

Hear from God

Use the letters from 'bread' to finish this sentence.

"_ _t this _s _ w_y of
_ _m_m _ _ _ing m_."

Gospels

Churches still share bread and wine to remember Jesus and his death. It's called 'Communion' or 'Eucharist' or 'the Lord's Supper'.

Jesus is arrested!

Have you ever known that something bad was going to happen, like a test or a nasty job you had to do? How did you feel while you were waiting for it? Would you have tried to get out of it if you could?

Read **Matthew 26:36–57**

True or false?

Jesus knew he would be arrested. **T/F**

Jesus wanted to be arrested. **T/F**

Think hard!

Judas was once Jesus' friend. **T/F**

Jesus could have stopped them from arresting him. **T/F**

Jesus was arrested because he'd committed a crime. **T/F**

Look at **Luke 22:1–6** to see the real reason why Jesus was arrested.

Gospels

Pilate questions Jesus

Imagine that you answered all the questions in a test perfectly, but when you got your marks you found that you'd failed the test and then you were punished for not working hard enough! How unfair!

Hear from God

Jesus' 'test' was unfair too…
Read **Luke 23:13–25**

Can you work out what Pilate said? Each letter has been changed to its Roman number. I=a, IV=d, V=e, VI=f, VII=g, VIII=h, IX=i, XII=l, XIII=m, XIV=n, XV=o, XX=t, XXI=u, XXII=v, XXV=y

IX   VIII I XXII V   XIV XV XX   VI XV XXI XIV IV

_____

VIII IX XIII   VII XXI IX XII XX XXV

_____

But Pilate was scared, so he handed over Jesus anyway.

Jesus is killed

Look back at page 38. The people were expecting Jesus to save them. So they must have thought it had all gone wrong when Jesus was put to death.

Hear from God

Read **Luke 23:33–49**, then finish the picture by adding the words.

Aren't you the Messiah?

Don't you fear God? ...We got what was coming to us,

THIS IS

Gospels

Now read **Luke 23:50–56**. Where was Jesus' body put?

Look back at pages 39 and 40. Had God's plan gone horribly wrong?

Think hard!

42

There's no-body there!

Although there's lots of evidence that Jesus lived and died just as the Gospels say, no one has ever found his body. But there's a very good reason for that!

Hear from God

Read **Mark 16:1–8** to see what it is. Can you spot eight differences between these two pictures?

Who were the people who saw Jesus on the day he came back to life…

In **John 20:11–16** _____
In **Luke 24:13–16** _____
In **Luke 24:36–39** _____

Where is Jesus now? (**Luke 24:50–53**)

_____

Gospels

God's Holy Spirit

Have you ever felt alone and in need of help? I do when I'm lost in a vast desert. When Jesus went back up to heaven, his disciples probably felt scared and alone. But God sent someone to help them.

Hear from God

Read **Acts 2:1–24**

God sent his Holy Spirit to help the disciples tell people about Jesus. Because of the Holy Spirit, people from all these places heard the disciples' message in their own languages. Can you find the places in the wordsearch?

I	L	M	P	A	R	T	H	I	A
R	C	R	A	I	G	Y	R	H	P
N	V	B	E	M	O	R	U	L	E
C	A	P	P	A	D	O	C	I	A
K	P	O	N	T	U	S	K	R	I
Q	G	S	R	O	P	F	W	A	B
K	P	A	M	P	H	Y	L	I	A
A	B	Y	N	O	X	L	G	I	R
G	S	B	K	S	J	U	D	E	A
C	O	I	F	E	T	E	R	C	W
Z	F	L	A	M	M	P	F	S	G

ARABIA
ASIA
CAPPADOCIA
CRETE
EGYPT
ELAM
JUDEA
LIBYA
MEDIA
MESOPOTAMIA
PAMPHYLIA
PARTHIA
PHRYGIA
PONTUS
ROME

From Saul to Paul

Not everybody listened to the disciples and joined the church, though. Some people, like Saul, tried to kill the followers of Jesus.

Read **Acts 9:1–19** to see what stopped Saul from trying to kill the Christians.

Who did Saul meet on the road? _____

After that, Saul was a changed man. He even changed his name from Saul to Paul. Change every 's' in this message to a 'p' to find out what Paul did after that.

Saul travelled from slace to slace sreaching and sraying for seosle to resent and believe. That made him unsosular with certain seosle who castured him and sut him in jail. But they couldn't srevent Saul from keesing in touch with sen and saser!

Some of Paul's letters

Most of the New Testament books are letters and a lot of them were written by Paul, even when he was in prison! Paul was an expert on the Bible and his letters help to explain why Jesus died and rose again.

Read **Colossians 2:13–15**

What did God nail to the cross? Write it on the picture.

Now read **Romans 3:23–26**.

We can come to God only through f _ _ _ _ in J_ _ _ _ _ .

Letters

More letters

The letters Romans and Colossians were written to the people in Rome and Colossae. But some letters are named after the person they were from instead of the person or people they were addressed to.

Decide whether these letters were **to** or **from** the person or people they are named after.

I Corinthians (1:2)   to or **from** Corinth?

Galatians (1:2)   to or **from** Galatia?

Ephesians (1:1)   to or **from** Ephesus?

Philippians (1:1)   to or **from** Phillipi?

I Thessalonians (1:1)   to or **from** Thessalonica?

I Timothy (1:2)   to or **from** Timothy?

Titus (1:4)   to or **from** Titus?

Philemon (v 1)   to or **from** Philemon?

Hebrews   to or **from** the Hebrews?

James (1:1)   to or **from** James?

I Peter (1:1)   to or **from** Peter?

3 John (v 1)   to or **from** John?

Jude (v 1)   to or **from** Jude?

Letters

John has a vision

The last book in the Bible is called Revelation, because it tells us about what God *revealed* to John in some visions. So it's a bit like the Prophecy books in the Old Testament.

What better way to finish off this notebook than with the last few verses of the last book in the Bible, from **Revelation 22:16–21**?

I am Jesus! And I am the one who sent my angel to tell you all these things for the churches. I am David's Great Descendant, and I am also the bright morning star…

The one who has spoken these things says, "I am coming soon!"

So, Lord Jesus, please come soon!

I pray that the Lord Jesus will be kind to all of you.

Take the words of the last sentence and make that your prayer to God.